The Publishers gratefully acknowledge assistance provided by Dr Lucinda Posset, Awake–Acting Vice Chair of the Association of Overtired Parents for her help while compiling this book.

Publishers: Ladybird Books Ltd., Loughborough
Printed in England. If wet, Italy.

'How it works'

THE
BABY

by J.A. HAZELEY, N.S.F.W.
and J.P. MORRIS, O.M.G.

(Authors of 'The Curious
Incident Of The Sleep In
The Night–Time')

A LADYBIRD BOOK FOR GROWN–UPS

This is a baby.

It cannot do much yet.

It cannot speak. It cannot move around. It cannot look after itself or keep itself clean.

And due to lack of sleep, nor can its parents.

For about forty weeks, a mother's body nurtures a growing life. Her body makes the chemicals she needs to prepare for the stress of motherhood.

The father's body nurtures a growing sense of panic instead. His body makes no helpful chemicals at all, so he buys some from the off-licence.

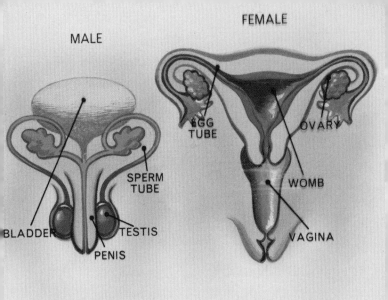

MALE

FEMALE

EGG
TUBE

OVARY

SPERM
TUBE

WOMB

BLADDER

TESTIS

PENIS

VAGINA

Above:

EMBRYO AT ONE
MONTH. ¼ INCH LONG.

Right:

FOETUS AT NINE
MONTHS. 20 INCHES.

Amber thinks her baby is the most beautiful baby in the whole world.

Unlike all other babies ever, this baby looks nothing like one of the Mitchell brothers dipped in purple ink and rancid yoghurt.

Amber cannot believe her luck.

How did she get the best one?

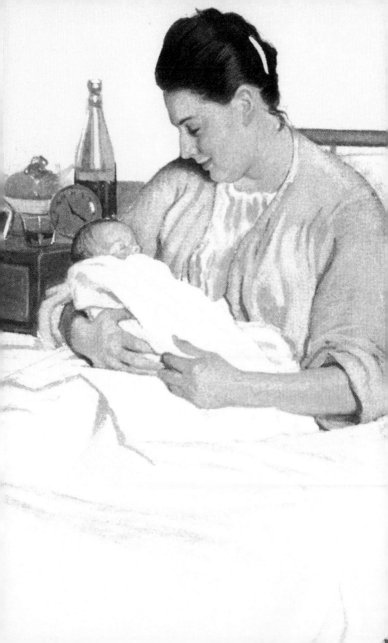

The hospital follows Jasmine's birth plan so she can have a drug-free delivery.

"I am glad it was all natural," shouts Jasmine, over the hissing and beeping and clanking and the hum of the lights.

Helena went to all the ante-natal and NCT classes she was offered. She wrote lots of lists. There was nothing she did not know about giving birth.

In the event, she was heavily sedated and missed most of it.

There are no classes at all about what to do next.

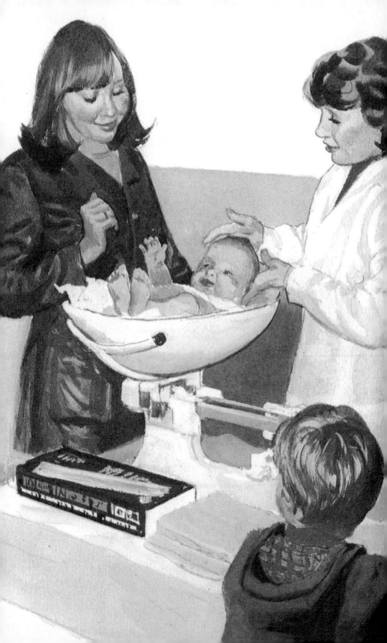

Before having a baby, it is a good idea to stock up on a few things.

Terry is packing his football, his boat, his model car collection, his vintage picture books, his Star Wars figures and his retro TV tie-in dolls into boxes. He is taking them to a storage unit.

His home office is going to be a nursery for the new baby.

Terry cannot believe his room will soon be full of kids' stuff.

Babies do not talk. They will not tell you what they want.

A parent has to listen for noises, be aware of smells, and look for when their child's face changes suddenly from happy to upset, if they want to avoid a nasty scene.

This stage is repeated at teenage.

What is that noise?

Is it cats fighting? Perhaps it is a dog. Or a fox in love.

Is it a car or a train? Might it be the wind or the boiler filling up?

Better go and see just in case. You can always sleep when your baby goes to university.

A baby has lots of clothes.

T-shirts for bands that the baby does not like yet. Snuggly hand-me-down snowsuits that are only the right size in summer.

And, even though a baby cannot walk, there are elaborate shoes. These are for kicking out of the push-chair so they can be hung from railings by strangers.

If baby Abigail eats all the food in the bowl, it will help her grow.

Her mum knows this because she usually absent-mindedly eats whatever Abigail leaves in the bowl, and she is definitely growing.

Since becoming a father, Den has been unable to watch any television or films featuring children in peril without bursting into tears.

Den was doing the recycling when he spotted a logo of a baby on a discarded bottle of washing–up liquid.

This may take some time.

There are three types of pram or push—chair.

The very big, safe one that you buy before you have your baby.

The tiny, flimsy one you buy after you have tried to get the big one onto a bus, that your in—laws worry about.

And the perfect one you buy two weeks before your baby stops needing a push—chair.

Charlotte has a whole shelf of baby care manuals.

Since having a baby, she has not had the time or energy to read any of them.

She has read "Boppy the Bear" though. Again and again and again.

All forty—six words of it.

The baby monitor is making a noise again.

"I don't care if I never sleep again," says Cally, "just as long as I die."

Many babies choose a favourite toy which they never want to be without.

This toy will be inexplicable, unwashable, impossible to replace through normal shops, easily thrown, dropped and lost, teeming with germs, and mainly in your child's mouth.

All Belinda's clothes are flecked with vomit. She has not slept for three days and has been wearing the same underwear for a week. She barely speaks to adults or leaves the house.

She loves her baby more than anyone in the whole world.

Hostage negotiators call this "Stockholm syndrome".

Sending your baby to nursery can help you get back to work.

There certainly is a lot of work to catch up on.

You can do it in bed, recovering from the many new bacterial and viral infections the baby brings home from nursery.

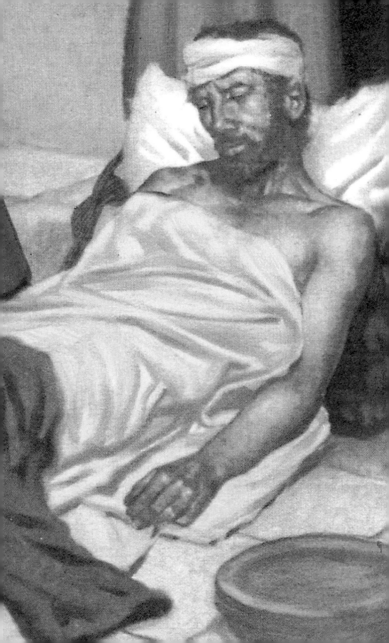

Olivia is trying to get Marvin to go down for his nap by taking him for a little drive.

Olivia runs out of petrol just as Marvin nods off.

Olivia tries to phone the AA but she does not know the code from Catalonia.

Allyce is taking Rainbeau to a local mother-and-baby group.

It takes her forty-five minutes to pack the bag with the change mat, nappies, wipes, nappy bags, Sudocrem, milk, muslins, teething powders, rice cakes, bibs, Calpol, spare clothes, dummies, first aid kit, Mr Bun-Bun and hand gel.

The play group is two minutes away.

Mike and Holly's usual baby—sitter was revising for an exam, so he called one he found on the advert wall at Asda.

The baby—sitter grabs the baby from Mike and dances round the garden, licking it.

"My baby! My baby! My baby!" she cackles.

Mike wishes he had called Holly's mum after all.

Fafnir enjoys cage fighting and Norwegian Black Metal. Pootle is a jazz clarinettist who spends his weekends restoring antique chessboards.

They have almost nothing in common, but their babies are roughly the same age, so they spend at least four mornings a week attempting conversation at playgroups, playgrounds and playdates.

It is mainly hell.

Penny will do anything to keep little Weymouth safe.

"I will never ever let you get hurt," she promises.

Within three months, Penny will have fallen down the stairs holding him twice, and cut off the end of his little finger with the nail scissors at least once.

Just like everyone does.

At the playground, Debbie is distracted from her phone by the sound of a small child crying.

"I hope that's not my child," she thinks, looking at Facebook.

"I'm sure one of the other mums will ring me if it is."

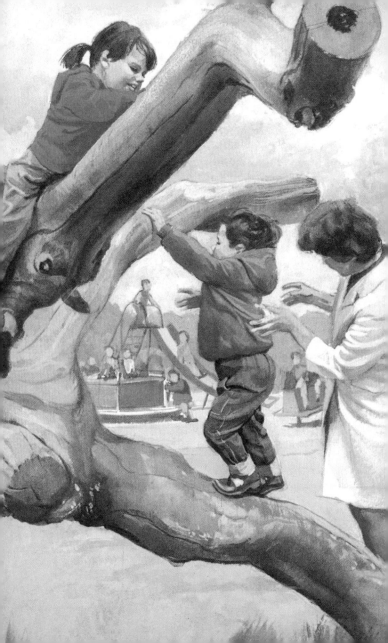

THE AUTHORS would like to record their gratitude and offer their apologies to the many Ladybird artists whose luminous work formed the glorious wallpaper of countless childhoods. Revisiting it for this book as grown-ups has been a privilege.

MICHAEL JOSEPH

UK | USA | Canada | Ireland | Australia
India | New Zealand | South Africa

Michael Joseph is part of the Penguin Random House group of companies whose addresses can be found at global.penguinrandomhouse.com

First published 2017
001

Copyright © Jason Hazeley and Joel Morris, 2017
All images copyright © Ladybird Books Ltd, 2017

The moral right of the authors has been asserted

Printed in Italy by L.E.G.O. S.p.A

A CIP catalogue record for this book is available from the British Library

ISBN: 978–0–718–18863–4

www.greenpenguin.co.uk

MIX
Paper from
responsible sources
FSC® C018179

Penguin Random House is committed to a sustainable future for our business, our readers and our planet. This book is made from Forest Stewardship Council® certified paper.